WHISPERS OF A YOUTHFUL SOUL

SIVANSH SATPATHY

Made with ♥ on the Notion Press Platform
www.notionpress.com

Contents

Contents

Prologue

In the realms of verse, a young heart's tale,
Where dreams unfurl and emotions set sail,
Amidst rhymes and rhythms, secrets reside,
A young adult's journey, with worlds to confide.
With ink as the guide, he paints life's array,
Experiences rendered, in verses that sway,
From soaring highs to depths unknown,
The essence of youth, in each poem sown.
They'll make you smile, inspire your soul,
Nudging you forward, to achieve your goal.
Yet not just sunshine graces the page,
For taboo realms, they do engage,
In life's philosophy, they find their stride,
Perspectives shaped, as they reflect and confide,
With nods of agreement, you'll find your way,
In the wisdom they share, day by day.
So, open this book, let your spirit soar,
In the world of a young soul's encore,
Their rhymes, their truths, like stars align,
As they share their heart, in each grand design.

1. Poems come through us

[This is a charming metapoetry by the young poet where he wonders who feels the truer emotion, the poet or the protagonist who has lived through the experience. Words can open different worlds for different people and enhance the experience.]

It dawned upon me when I read
A poem that was quite well said
Twas titled "if "by Rudyard Kipling
I found it on the poster, owned by my sibling

When I understood it at last
And looked into my past
I felt like it was meant for me
But did he feel it as much as me? Did he?

Does a poet always feel
The message he did seal
More than someone who had read every part
And had felt it so closely in his heart

I realised it may not always be the case
It's a fact we poets learn to face
Our verses are made for you
That's why they are about the things you do

Poems come through us, not from us
So, poets don't read this and fuss
As we both know we don't understand our poems as well
As the men whose stories we tell

2. This is your chance

[A reflection of life by a dying soul, this poignant poem will surely inspire, as well as make you sigh. The protagonist is stuck in a gorge and as his life force is ebbing away, he gets a flashback of all that he has lived through and all that he wanted to achieve in this life but now cannot. He urges the reader to learn from his own life and not repeat these mistakes as life can be taken away from one when he least expects it.]

It was a sunny day on a beautiful gorge
A time for peace and happiness to forge
It did until I got stuck
In deep waters, oh what luck!
I saw my life from start to end
And saw how each moment I did spend
Since when I could remember
From January to December
till now this very moment
All I can do is repent
In this I lay restless, ever so helpless
I promised myself from this day
Now's the time" is what I will say
If I ever see the light of day
But as for me, my tomorrow may never come
All I wish, is that I had fun,
I can't now, but you can have some
I will live like there is only today
For tomorrow may not come, but that's okay
As whatever I wanted to do I did
They way I used to behave as a kid
But in vain, this chance won't come again
Even if it does, the excuse stays the same
On why you neglected your dreams when opportunity came
I lay here in wait for death to arrive
But as for you, you're still alive
If you are reading this, there is still hope

Don't look at chance and be like "Nope"
THIS is your chance
Your life you can still enhance
Take control of your life now
Make it so beautiful, others ask , how
My end has come at last
I have more to say, so I'll say it fast
Just live now, forget your past
Keep learning, for knowledge is vast

3. Yeh Dil Mange More

[An ode to a braveheart soldier who gave the ultimate sacrifice while fighting for his country in the Kargil war. It talks about how soldiers desire to serve their nation.]

In our world of courage and cowardice
We are often fooled by people in disguise
Although not many,
some men leave a legacy

Such as Vikram Batra
Who was awarded the Paramveer Chakra
For his outstanding relentlessness
And for operating with such finesse

After killing eight soldiers
He radioed his command post
Despite being tired and sore
He says" yeh dil maange more"

Despite the pain
Our brave captain in vain
Crawls towards the enemy
And performs tasks considered impossible in the military

A man who fought so laboriously
With such outstanding bravery
A man who fought till there was no breath in his lung
Is a man great enough for his songs to be sung

Such men are hard to find
Who are fierce yet still be kind
A man who walks through flames and not get burnt
We know their names long after they leave the earth

4. A Poem's sensibility

[This poem talks about how poets intend to send a particular message through their poem but ultimately it's the reader who interprets it. This is how the same poem can mean very different things to different people, including the poet and the reader]

A poem may have infinite interpretations,
As there are infinite ways to think;
Despite the poet's proclamations,
The message that will sink;

Depends on he who reads it,
Not the poet's will;
For it will involve the reader's wit,
The poet has no control on that, nil.

5. Nightfall

[A teenage boy experiencing nightfall for the first time goes through a myriad of emotions, however, he learns from this experience as well. The poet tells us nightfall is just another life process and should be treated as such; no regrets or penance required.]

I woke up and I didn't feel so great
I looked down and realised, I was late
I felt my pants so wet
'there's something on me', did it set?
I look down and see a stain on my pant
This cant be true, it just cant!

I tell myself it's a dream
Its harder to sleep after that, than it may seem
When I get up from my sleep
I pull up the cover to take a peep
"Oh God! Its still there!"
Why did God do this to me? It isn't fair
No point to cry now
I try to fix this but I don't know how

Do I deal with this
white sticky annoying piss
I rush to the bathroom
I feel like this will be my doom
Heaters on now, but it will probably take
Half an hour, hope it gets hot fast for God's sake

Of course there's no towel and the water's still cold

But when the going gets tough, the tough get going , I was told
So I keep going and to myself I say
We're gonna get through this , okay
God was listening at that time
I guess he paid attention to the rhyme
Suddenly I saw the towel on the shelf
And I decided to help myself

I stepped in the bath fingers crossed
Turned on the shower and then paused
Expecting cold water, the water was warm
I came out refreshed
Got my favourite clothes and then got dressed
You see I realised something that day

I'll tell you now if I may
Nightfall can only make you sad if you let it
But if you don't waste time by crying, you won't regret it

6. Life will pass you by

[This is an inspirational poem with a powerful message. We often go through life planning about the future when all we should be doing is having fun in the present moment. If we could just live in the present moment, then we would live an enriching and deeply fulfilling life.]

What will you do before you die?
Or will you let life pass you by?
What moment are you waiting for?
For opportunity wont knock at your door
For when you're old and sore?
When do you plan to have fun
When all your work is done?
Who told you such a day would come
Or are you just dumb?
We both know there's always work to do
I know and so do you
When will you realise? When your time is done
That no matter what you do, time and tide wait for none
So listen very carefully, for I shall tell this once
Only for I am your father
And you are my generation's son
Rich or poor, your life is one
And it may soon be done
After money don't run, my dear son
Coz it's just paper at the end
What use of it if you don't spend
I'm not asking you not to work
Simply for you to enjoy its perk
Rather have fun while you work
Just don't let sadness lurk
For again I emphasise
Don't live in lies

You will die and never again be born
No matter how much your family may mourn
So, don't waste your time by cry
For then life will pass you by
Don't live in a lie
For then life will pass you by
Don't let what others say
Ruin your day
Don't mind fitting into society
If you have to completely change who you are
Don't forget what I said, so lets summarise what I said by far
So my son, live before you die
Or life will pass you by
Or life will pass you by

7. The truth of war

[The poet's philosophy on war is evident in this poem. The poet laments the futility of war and the bloodshed it causes. According to the poet, all this is meaningless and he wonders if only people thought through things before taking action, the conflicts of the world could be resolved]

Battles aren't fought to resolve conflicts
They are to send a message, just one
Battles have been lost,

But name one that's been won

Battles are for revenge
They waste the lives of some
Battles kill innocents
And plead death to come

Battles don't cause benefit
They kill everyone
Battles cause grieving
Ask anyone

It doesn't matter who won or lost
For lives were taken away
It's a sin to humanity
For men fought their brothers and here their bodies lay

There have been a billion battles
And there will be billions more
Why men still fight, I don't know for
Its never resolved anything before

Poor soldiers die
Their families cry
I don't know why war exists
Countries fight on who's right
But the problem persists

Why even bother
When one fight causes another
But in disdain,
Our human brain can't resist
To think a little before, we return a fist
But if we didn't act as quick and thought for just a bit
We could avoid the whole problem, now that's called wit.

But peace is just a fantasy
Never to come true
We will continue to beat each other
Till we're black and blue

But when we realise all we beat
Is ourselves, it'd be too late
To stop this stupidity disguised as glory
For then it'd be up to fate

For we'll be dead
And you'll repent
That you hadn't listened
To what I had said

8. The beast

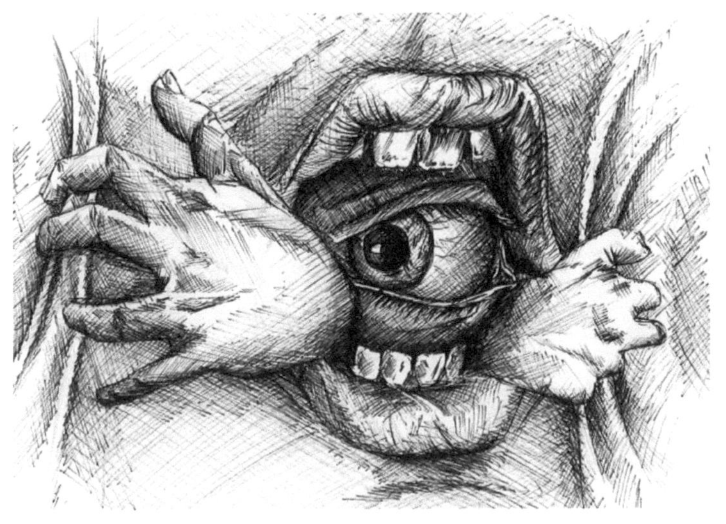

[A poem about the inner struggles we go through when we face our fears or don't stand up to them]

Its dark and scary with eyes so bright
It's out to get me, I know I'm right
It's in my path and refuses to leave
If I turn back my fate will seal
I'll never get on this path again
For my problem I didn't deal
So with my inner voice I made my choice
My heart beating fast but constantly
To fight with the weapons I had
I lost and fell but more importantly,
I got up and told you're fighting me
You pushed me down but I don't give up easy

9. Blood sweat and tears

[This poem reinstates the importance of hard work and consistency and why we should keep going even in the face of adversity]

You need hope, craze, and pain
For anything to gain
You need blood sweat and tears
To face all your fears
Live life with no regrets
No matter how hard it gets
For pain is an ant I bet
If an elephant were regret
The pain of a missed opportunity
Stays forever in the heart
For you'll realise years from now
When it'd be too late to start
You could have worked your way to the top
Now you are at the bottom, going lower, with no way to stop

10. Organ Donation

[A heart wrenching poem about organ donation, the poet hopes to inspire everyone to donate their organs]

When I die, take my organs as I lie
Coz I ain't using it no more
So I give it to you to try
As I say bye, you'll be saying "hi"
For you have a new shot at life
Have a nice one with a house and a wife

And don't think its something great that I am doing
They'll burn or decompose anyways and end in ruin
I mean, what will I do with my organs when I am gone
Instead I can give it to you so at least you can see the light of dawn
That I'll never see, but that's okay
But its my eyes, so I'll see it you could say

Oh! And take my liver too
I hardly ever drink so its good as new
But that probably ain't the case for you
Got Cirhosis? It hurts when you go to the loo
But now you've another shot
To live the fullest with what you just got

Oh! And don't forget to take my heart
That's probably the most important part
Don't worry, it doesn't get tired
That's why its admired
Take care of it
Don't let another stroke hit

I gave you my heart before I went above
So its filled with good wishes and love
Take my kidneys and pancreas too
Give it to someone else, if it isn't useful to you

11. 4 that kid

[This is a poem on perseverance and what it takes to be brave in the face of criticism. It is dedicated to all those people who have never let their deficiencies stand in their way, but have succeeded out of sheer perseverance]

This rhyme's for that kid
Who has been called weak, dumb, stupid
The one who just can't get it right
No matter the opposition, he stands up to fight

He works so hard but he's still behind
People make fun of him but he doesn't mind
Doesn't matter if you forget his name
Coz he does it for him, not for fame

Do what you want, but he can't be stopped
Coz he's already failed and flopped
He knows he may never be the best
But until he does it, he can't rest

When he dies he won't go to heaven or hell
He'll become a legend who's story I tell

12. I didn't like storms and rain

[This is an endearing poem of a boy who is scared of rain till he discovers how beautiful rain can be. At a deeper level, the rain and storm is a metaphor for all things that are unknown and hence feared, but if one takes a bit of effort, one can truly see beauty in everything]

I didn't like storms and rain
A little boy was I
I asked mum why rain exists
Why mummy why
I would sit in a corner until the rain died
And all I would do is cry, cry and cry
I pulled the covers over me and there I would lie

I was once home alone when I was fourteen
But I was still scared and I would scream
There was stiffness in the air and thunder in my heart
From the window the white light would beam
I didn't quite know why I was afraid

And decided to peep
The sight I saw is a memory I still keep
It was scary, well more than that, to face my fear
As for me, I felt my end was near

But using the courage I did not have, I step outside to meet

the rain
Oh and what a gentleman he is!
His wind steal my heat and in return provide a cool breeze
My frustration senses an emotion it will cease

His steady patter and unpredictable thunder
Is music to my ears, and makes me surrender
His sweet smell of wet earth cant be quantified on worth
For tis the scent of water air and earth.

His appearance can only make you smile
The prettiest of people will be off by a mile
His touch is gentle and fills me with goodness
But if you make him angry he'll mess

If he comes too much I'd drown till my last breath
But If he doesn't come at all it would be certain death
Oh I remember the day we met
I Thought you'd be the one I'd never get

Long back If I hadn't had that peep
Oh I can't imagine how much I'd weep
If I'd never taken a chance with you
Oh what would I do
Oh what would I do

13. Our world Would not exist

[An innocent poem about our world, with a stark message for all of us at the end. The poem talks about how our world would not exist mentally, spiritually, and physically]

If a giraffe was small
and a mouse was tall
Our world would not exist

if I weren't born
and you were gone
Our world would not exist

If sun didn't vomit earth
and earth had not taken birth
Our world would not exist

If our rule stays
And we don't change our ways
OUR WORLD WILL NOT EXIST

14. Stars in a cloudy sky

[This metaphorical poem tells us how our dreams are clearly visible when we are focussed and have clarity of thought but sometimes failures can cloud our judgement and demotivate us. However, we should still carry on with the faith that our dreams are still within our reach]

When you look at the starry skies
You want to touch the stars
But on a cloudy day
You feel like you're behind bars
Seeing no stars , you stop dreaming
But my dear don't rely on feeling
Though the sky is bare
The stars are still there
Behind the clouds peeping
Their light still beaming

15. Results don't matter when

[This is a motivational poem that teaches us the prize of pain. It talks about the people who try very hard at something but still fail, but despite this they continue pursuing their craft relentlessly. The protagonist in the poem tries his level best to get what he desires but inspite this he fails to do so, while others who didn't put nearly enough effort as him got what he desired simply because of natural skill and luck. The protagonist doesn't shed a tear though despite his failure rather he is proud. Unlike those who didn't

work as hard but got through who are feeling guilty. He says this is because those who got by natural talent and luck owe their victory to god as without god's help they would be nothing. But the poet on the other hand delt with all the difficulties and didn't get help from God but continued to work despite no one being on his side]

When you can work on something you hate
When you can finish everything on your plate
When you don't feel like it but do it all the same
When you try harder than anyone and lose but still stay in the game
When you can sacrifice the thing you love
When you don't need the person above
When you can push despite the pain
Fail a thousand times and try again
When you can go one when no one believes in you
From family friends the Gods too
When you have been called stupid by everyone you know
When you push even when you're at the lowest of the low
When you can do this the results won't matter
Even if all your hopes and dreams shatter
Cause no matter what anyone else say
You can be like listen, okay?
I'm the last? Well I don't care
Cause I worked harder than anyone else there
By seeing your face I can tell
That you all know it well

Now you're feeling guilty with your college degree
And I am feeling pride, how can that be?
See you got by, by your natural talent
You didn't do much work just played Valorant
I didn't have no talent still I grind
I didn't get nothing but I don't mind
WHY? Cause you owe it to God, but on your own you'd die
Cause you wouldn't be able to do anything but complain and cry
But ME , Even though no one was on my side
I did my best that's my pride
That's a feeling you'll never know
No matter how rich or far you go

16. I knew not how to read

[This is a poem about hidden talent. it says talent is of no use if not shown to others. For example, if someone has the talent of juggling but doesn't show it to others his talent is useless . The

protagonist is unable to read and hence, even though he might be surrounded by a thousand books, he cannot avail the knowledge in them]

I gazed upon a thousand books
I knew not how to read
I looked inside and found a rhyme
I knew not how to read
Timeless wisdom before me
I knew not how to read
I sat down and pondered for long of what the song could mean
Though the rhyme had immense wisdom it was no use to me
What use of talent if not shown to thee

17. Why your dreams won't come true

[Another inspirational poem, this is sure to fire you up when you are feeling down and out and feel like giving up on your dreams. Reading this will help you get back on your feet and get going]

Don't wait, just don't
Your dreams wont just come true, it won't
If you have a problem no one will give you the solution
The ruse that if you pray to God it'll come, is just an illusion

The truth is no one likes work, trust me I know
But great men don't care they just go
It doesn't matter if you're on top
Or you're the one they call a flop

What matters is that you put in the work everyday
Working hard. No play, sacrifice there's a price you pay
Don't matter if you like your work or not
Work with whatever you got

Feel sad, too bad, still I work
Wanna play? NOT today still I work
Wanna cry, wanna die, still I work
Why? Cause life won't ask what you feel like

People will say things will work out , Sike!
Is what they'll say when you realize
That you've been living in lies
HUH! You'll say where success at?
It's with the guy who worked for that
But hey he ain't as smart as me

True but he worked harder you see
B-b-b-ut I prayed all the time and waited for the right time

I'm smarter than he is but he took my spot that's a crime !
TSK, TSK said the guy at success
You know how I took your spot, can't you guess?
You may be smarter and you maybe stronger

But I worked harder and I worked longer
So while you were whining and crying
I worked so hard, practically dying
That's why there's a difference between me and you
Its only because of the things we do
Like by reading this rhyme and learning about work in large amounts
YOU REALISE ITS NOT WHERE YOU START BUT THE FINISH THAT COUNTS!

18. In a class I wondered

[It is a nostalgic poem that takes us back to our youth. It talks about all the sorts of things going through a small child's mind in his classroom. It shows how fast, creative, and random a child's thinking processes is. It also throws light on how a child can think of such deep thoughts but yet no one gives any value for his thoughts. He also thinks of thoughts that people might consider silly but are often real questions of life. While other thoughts he has, have a much deeper meaning than they seem. This teaches us not to take anyone for granted]

What use of the teacher teaching, when no one seems to be listening
What use of holidays if you have work to do
What use of speaking if you can't listen too
What use of money when you don't want to use it
What use of the "hour" when you have the "minute"
What use of books if they aren't read
What use of the body without the head
What use of planning when you can't predict the future
What use of sowing a seed when you don't know how to nurture
What use of a pleasant body without a pleasant mind
What use of the Mona Lisa if you'r blind
What use of what others think when you have your life to live
What use of owning everything when you don't know how to give
What use of ever learning if I were to forget
What use of giving when I can get

19. Why you should become veg according to a chicken

[This is a humorous poem that describes the world from a chicken's point of view and also points out the inherent hypocrisy in human beings]

Wait! Don't eat me!
I may be a chicken but you're a meanie
When I was young, I was well fed
I thought you were nice but now you want me dead?
You were like "off with his head"
That's exactly what you said
Before you ripped my clothes so
You could hang me up for show
Then someone will come over one of these days
Give me a leg piece he says
Then casually my leg you rip
While your friend smacks his lip
Then you tear the flesh with my skin
Don't you feel guilty while you sin
You like to preach don't you
"Don't harm animals" you say
You act like some angel too
Then recollect what you did today

20. Why You should become veg according to a cow

[Another light hearted attempt from a cow's point of view to inspire the reader to give up beef!]

I was just chewing on a leftover snack
That I had eaten a while back
It was warm and had a chewy feel
Oh, how I love this delicious meal
Then suddenly I spot John
He looks at me and says my youth is gone
He takes me to a tall building called slaughter house
As we reach he goes as quiet as a mouse

It looks quite nice with the fields behind it
Unlike John who looks wretched with
A clearly sad face filled with tears
The day has come that he fears
He has been real nice to me
So him like this I cant see
I lick his ear playfully and lay my head in his hand
He hugs me and says warily he loves me and
He's doing this for money and doesn't like this at all
Is what he says as his tears fall
He leaves me at the gate
Where I would seal my fate
A big hand reaches out and drags me inside
I look in the "house" and almost died
Seeing the million carcases of my brothers on the floor
Soon I will too be waiting on heaven's door

So that I can give some stranger pleasure who I have never met before
But that stranger won't even think of me he will just ask for more
The more they ask the more we die
The more you laugh the more we cry
So continue to kill my friends
Or you could choose to make amends
You have killed my mom and dad, a sin
But you can choose not to kill my kin
The choice is yours, a life of guilt
Or a life of honour, well built

21. Intrusive thoughts

[This poem addresses this generation's ill and talks of dark depressive thoughts that one might feel at any point in life. The poem suggests a very simple way to tackle them from his point of view]

Have you ever felt alone?
Deep in thoughts of your own
Feelings that can't be expressed as such
Coming in waves, a bit too much
From all the thoughts that cross your mind
Pick the worst ones you can find
Allow yourself to feel them through
Now tell each one "I'll never do you".

22. What do I see?

[This is a silly poem about a young child, describing what he sees in various things. He gets so lost in thought he loses all sense of time. He first starts daydreaming in the morning while he gets ready for school. Then as he sits in class he daydreams as he looks out the window. When he comes back home and sits down to do his homework he is still deep in thought. He continues to think at night until he is met with a surprise!]

I look into the mirror and what do I see?
I see a boy staring acting like he is me !

I look into the sky and what do I see?
I see white figures that look like cotton candy!

I look into my book and what do I see?
I see some black letters like ABCD!

I look at the clock, it's 12:03
I see one hand at twelve and the other at three!

I look into my mum's face and what do I see?
It's past midnight and she is angry!

23. A Letter to Santa

[This poem was written at the onset of Covid and the lockdown, when kids were cooped up in their homes and turned to Santa for rescue!]

Dear Santa,
I must request
to take that pest
That corona virus thing
It has disturbed our, very existing
I need to live and play
And not be home all day
All video games are now lame
Cause they all feel the same
My eyes hurt seeing that screen
Oh how long it's been
And for the hundredth time, I don't want to be bored to death
It must be fun to roam around and not just stay in bed
So please gift us the vaccine
And that I truly mean

24. GenAI, Oh What to SAY

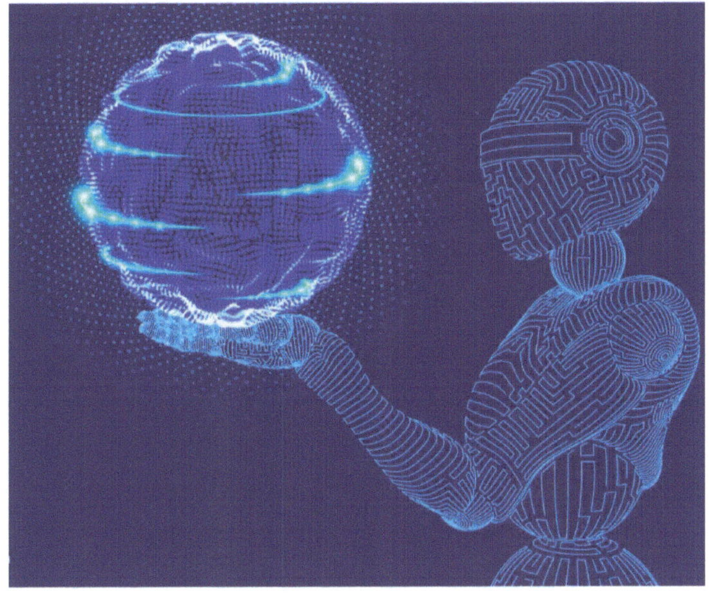

[This poem takes a pragmatic view of GenAI and how it can affect our lives if we let it]

GenAI oh what to say!
Is making our generation dumber by the day
The more you use it the smarter it grows
All your information it knows
It stores your information well
And who knows to whom it may sell
It keeps a file on all that you type
So I don't get all the hype
Of losing your security and integrity too
When your words aren't written by you
"But it's fast and easy to use!"
Is what idiots say before they lose
Their job , reputation and value
Because they made chatgpt do
The work they were supposed to
And their work was taken by you know who
The one they thought helped them grow
Now they're the ones who have to bow
Down to the monster they have awoken
Left them helpless ever so broken

25

25. What could you be?

(An inspirational poem to make you really think of all that you could accomplish in life if only you let yourself)

What do you do when it can't be done
When it gets hard and stops being fun
What do you do when left astray
Deep in thought, can't find your way
Do you turn back and run away?
Or fight to try another way?
Do you waste your time in thinking?
Or do you find a way to stop sinking
Where would you be, if you chose the other choice
Would you be sad or would you rejoice
Who would you be if you saw through their eyes,
Would you be you, or a man in disguise
What could you be if you gave it your all
Would you be happy even if you fall
Who, where
and what could you be
Please find out, we'd like to see!

www.ingramcontent.com/pod-product-compliance
Lightning Source LLC
LaVergne TN
LVHW021341160826
845679LV00008B/1438

* 9 7 9 8 8 9 1 3 3 3 4 4 4 *